THE WORLDVIEW OF HERMAN GRIMM

In Relation to Spiritual Science

Rudolf Steiner

From Rudolf Steiner: *Ergebnisse der Geistesforschung*

(Some Results of Spiritual Research)

GA 62. Lecture VIII, 16th January 1913 in Berlin

Translated by Peter Stebbing

First Printing

Rudolf Steiner Publications

This is a lecture, given by *Rudolf Steiner*, entitled *Herman Grimm und die Geistesforschung* and contained in the volume *Ergebnisse der Geistesforschung* (Results of Spiritual Research) GA 62.

Cover designed by Peter Stebbing
Cover photo by Alma Lessing, © SLUB Dresden
Deutsche Fotothek / Martin Würker (reproduction)
"Anthros" lettering: Peter Zeswitsch

Lecture Translated by Peter Stebbing

Editing by James D. Stewart
e.Librarian at the
Rudolf Steiner Archive & e.Lib
Visit the website at https://www.rsarchive.org/

The "I" Initial graphic was designed by Rudolf Steiner

Printed in the United States of America

Paperback: ISBN-13 978-1-948302-15-9
ISBN-10 1-948302-15.2
Kindle: ISBN-13: 978-1-948302-14-2
ISBN-10: 1-948302-14-4

"Spiritual science aims to show what can be gained in widening one's spiritual horizons. It can be said that for the purpose of gradually entering into the whole outlook inherent in spiritual research, anyone immersing himself in Herman Grimm's spirit has the finest precepts."

Rudolf Steiner, GA 62

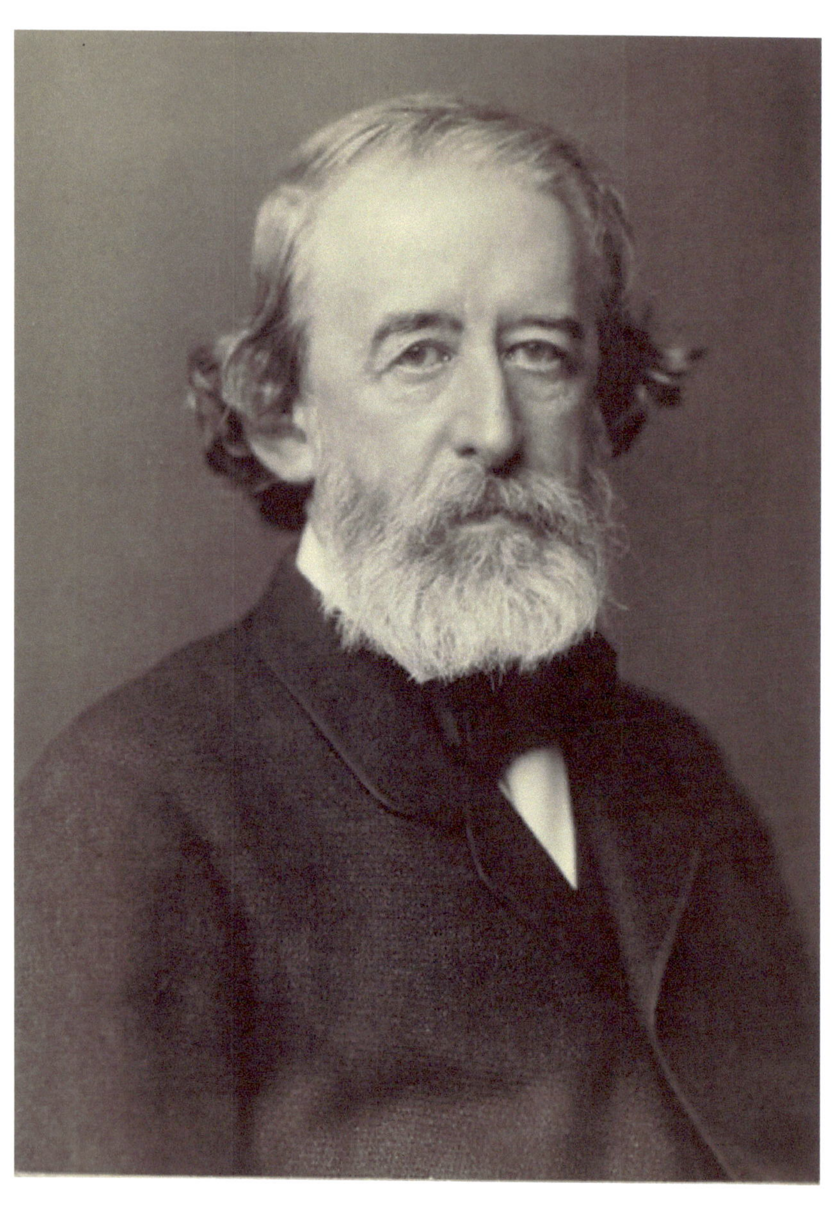

Herman Grimm

THE WORLDVIEW OF HERMAN GRIMM

In Relation to Spiritual Science

Rudolf Steiner

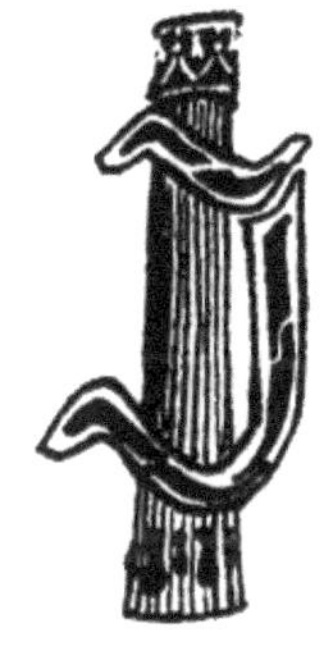

t could easily appear as though what is set forth here as spiritual science stood in isolation to what is otherwise proclaimed and of a tone-setting nature in the cultural life of the present. However, it can only appear so to one who conceives of this spiritual science in a somewhat narrow-hearted sense, seeing in it nothing more than a sum of teachings and theories. On the other hand, whoever recognizes it as a spiritual stream open to new sources will become aware that parallels can be drawn to modern cultural life in various ways. It will be seen that this manner of viewing life called spiritual science can be applied to other, in some degree related directions. A direction of this sort is the subject of to-day's considerations — as represented by a prominent personality of modern cultural life, the art historian and researcher *Herman Grimm*.

Herman Grimm [the son of Wilhelm Grimm of the

Brothers Grimm] was born in 1828 and died in 1901. He appears indeed as a quite characteristic figure of modern life, and yet he is, at the same time, so distinctive and unique as to stand apart. Today's considerations can connect especially well onto this personality. To anyone having occupied himself with Herman Grimm, he appears as a kind of mediator between all that relates to Goethe, and to our own spiritual life.

By reason of his marriage to the daughter of a personality, who stood close to the circle of Goethe, namely the sister of the romantic poet [*Clemens von*] *Brentano, Bettina Brentano* [1785-1859], Herman Grimm was connected in a quite special sense with everything associated with the name of Goethe. Herman Grimm was related to her in that she was his mother-in-law, the same Bettina Brentano who had brought out Goethe's remarkable exchange of letters with a child. Bettina Brentano's unique memorial shows us Goethe enthroned like an Olympian, a musical instrument in his hands, while she presents herself as a child grasping at the strings. From the Frankfurt circle of La Roche, in her relation to Goethe she was able (like few others) to enter into Goethe's spirit. Even if some things as presented in the letters are inexact, being colourfully mixed together in various ways — a combination of poetry and truth — it still has to be said: Everything in this remarkable book,

Goethes Briefwechsel mit einem Kinde [*Goethe's Exchange of Letters with a Child*], grew in a heartfelt manner out of sensing Goethe's whole outlook. In a wonderful way, it grants us an echo of his wisdom-imbued worldview. Bettina Brentano was married to the poet *Achim von Arnim* [1781-1831], who had contributed to bringing out the fine collection of folk poems called *Des Knabens Wunderhorn* [1806] [*The Boy's Magic Horn*]. By virtue of the connection with this circle — as mentioned, *Gisela Grimm*, Herman Grimm's wife, was one of the daughters of Bettina von Arnim — Herman Grimm grew up from youth onwards, as it were, amid personalities who stood in close proximity to Goethe. In all that he took up in his education, Herman Grimm absorbed something of an immediate, elemental spiritual breath of Goethe. Thus, he felt himself as belonging to all those who had stood personally close to Goethe, even though he was still a child at the time of Goethe's death [in 1832J, rather than as one who had "studied" Goethe and Goetheanism. Herman Grimm counted as having taken into himself, in a direct and personal way, something of Goethe's essential being, his magical power, his natural humanity.

With inner participation, Herman Grimm experienced the development of German cultural life during the decades of the mid-nineteenth century. In doing so, he established, so to say, his own "kingdom" within this German cultural life. He can be called a spirit who, in an individual manner, starts out from whatever stimulated him and furthered the development of his own powers. In this way, out of the whole range of cultural life, a realm subdivided itself for Herman Grimm that suited his aims, a realm in which he felt at home. Within this domain in which Herman Grimm felt himself at home, he understood himself to be, so to say, the spiritual "governor" with respect to Goethe. Goethe's spirit appeared to him as though it lived on. And in seeking out what derived from Goethe and what was compatible with him in cultural life, entering into this, it was always the essence of Goethe that he sought. This then became a yardstick for him in evaluating everything in cultural life.

These were decades of struggle in German cultural life, decades in which everything to do with Goethe receded, following his death. So much else of immediate everyday concern stood in the forefront, rather than what proceeded from Goethe. During that period, numerous other things asserted themselves in the cultural life of Germany, while little was heard of Goethe. On account of his connection with Goethe, Herman Grimm regarded himself as one whose task it was, quietly yet actively to cultivate and carry over Goethe's ethos to a future time that he certainly hoped would come, a time in which Goethe's star would shine out once more in the European spiritual firmament.

In that he regarded himself as, so to say, the "governor" of Goethe's spiritual domain, Herman Grimm stood somewhat apart in his relation to cultural matters. It seemed appropriate, if not self-evident to see him as having the air of a "lord." Even in his stature, his physiognomy, his gestures, in his conduct, there was something about him suggestive of an aristocrat. And, it can be said: For anyone not accustomed to looking up to someone as to a lordly personality, Herman Grimm's whole demeanour as though compelled acknowledgement of the aforementioned status. I still fondly recall being together with Herman Grimm in Weimar, which he often liked to visit. On one occasion, he invited me as his only guest to a midday meal. We spoke about various matters that interested him. We also talked — and I was pleased that he wanted to have this conversation with me — about his comprehensive life-plans. And when a certain time had passed after the meal, he said, in his inimitable, humorous and quite natural manner, such that one accepted it from him as something innate, "Now, my dear Doctor, I wish graciously to dismiss you!" As though a matter of course, it actually made a self-evident impression on me. And it accorded with Herman Grimm's whole manner of conducting himself, so that, one granted him a certain air of lordliness.

Herman Grimm's whole lifework bears something of the same attribute. One cannot take up one of his major or minor writings, with their harmonious and so succinctly constructed sentences without feeling: all this affects one as though the author's personality stood behind it, regarding one with soulful participation. This contributes to the wonderful quality in Herman Grimm's writings. In every respect they are the product of his soul-imbued personality and have their immediate effect as such. In this way, his style takes on a certain justified, noble pathos. However, this noble pathos is mitigated everywhere by the individual, human element that breaks through. One accepts his style despite its elegance. Everywhere, one senses his origins in having sincerely absorbed Goethe's spirit. Yet this is not all; it becomes apparent that with him the Goethean element has undergone something of the development of German Romanticism. We sense in Herman Grimm's style a liberation from all that can broadly be termed "commonplace" or "customary." We have the impression of a singular personality secluded within himself.

Herman Grimm's orientation could possibly have led to a certain one-sidedness, had something else not played a part, binding him closely to tradition; Herman Grimm was, after all, the, son of *Wilhelm Grimm* and the nephew of *Jakob Grimm*. Known for inaugurating modern linguistic research, these two collected the German fairy tales that have in the meantime profoundly permeated German life. They listened to the sagas and fairy tales told them by simple folk, that were almost forgotten and remembered by only a few remaining souls. Brought to life again by the Brothers Grimm, they now live on.

Despite a refined style in everything he produced, Herman Grimm also had close ties to popular tradition, combining this with what might otherwise have been a one-sided direction. We still have to stress something further by which he appears harmonious and complete. In taking up the works of Herman Grimm, we encounter something of his adaptability — a capacity to connect with the various spiritual phenomena in which he immersed himself in the course of his life. A certain isolation is required for someone to submerge themselves fully in the phenomena and facts of past centuries. This adaptability, this quality of "softness" with regard to Herman Grimm acquires its "skeleton," however, its necessary "hardness," by reason of something else that intervened in his upbringing. Both his father and his uncle belonged to the "Göttingen Seven," who in the year 1837 submitted their proclamation protesting the abolition of their country's constitution. They were consequently expelled from the

University of Göttingen. Thus, already as a child, Herman Grimm experienced a significant event and its aftermath. For there were consequences both for his father and his uncle, in that they not only lost their positions, but their daily bread as well at the time. Herman Grimm often referred to how he had experienced historical change in this way, even already as a nine-year old boy, and not merely via book-learning.

At a time when little was said of Goethe in Germany, attention having been diverted to other things, Herman Grimm viewed himself as a representative of Goethe's ethos. But he did experience a resurgence of interest in Goethe and was himself able to contribute to it. At the beginning of the seventies of the nineteenth century, he was able to hold his famous Goethe lectures ["Goethe-Vorlesungen" 1874-75] at the University of Berlin, also published in book form. Anyone getting hold of it as a young person, and able to find the right relation to it, will undoubtedly speak of it in later years as being of special significance. And, as set forth in this book, Herman Grimm clearly shows himself as someone who knew the various ramifications of Goethe's soul life.

We gain a clear sense of how Herman Grimm viewed a personality such as Goethe. We find nothing of a small-minded biographical compulsion — to flush out all manner of more or less indifferent traits. Rather do we find an immersion in everything that was important for Goethe's development — the endeavour to pursue what Goethe experienced in life, what lived in his soul, and how this re-constituted itself, taking on form to become a creation of Goethe's phantasy. How, he asks, in forgetting everything of a particular life experience, did this re-arise for Goethe to become the product of creative phantasy — a new experience?

Thus, in Herman Grimm's interpretation, Goethe raises his life-experiences a stage higher, to a sphere of pure spiritual contemplation. We see Goethe ascend to spiritual experiences. Herman Grimm demonstrates this with regard to each of Goethe's works. And we gladly follow him in pursuing this course, since with Herman Grimm nothing intrudes that can otherwise so easily enter into such a portrayal — that a single soul-force, e.g., reason or phantasy, becomes paramount, as it were, and one no longer feels the connection to immediate life. Herman Grimm goes no farther than he can go as an individual in contemplating Goethe's work. In the end, we are led by Herman Grimm to the point where the work takes its start from Goethe's life experience. One feels oneself transported everywhere into unmitigated spiritual life. Goethe becomes a sum of spiritual impulses. This breath of the spiritual extends throughout Herman Grimm's Goethe book.

What Herman Grimm ascribed to Goethe in this

way has its roots deep in Herman Grimm's spiritual configuration. Long before commencing these considerations that led to his lectures on Goethe, a grand, a colossal idea had stood before him — the idea of viewing occidental cultural life as a whole in the same way he had done, individually, with regard to Goethe. The idea stood before his mind's eye of following three millennia of western cultural life so as to reveal everywhere how human sensibility transforms everyday events in the physical world to what the human soul experiences upon ascending to the realm of "creative phantasy," as Herman Grimm called it. Thus, he becomes a unique kind of historian. For Herman Grimm, history was, so to say, something altogether different from what it is for other modern historians.

History is, after all, customarily studied in that documents, materials, are first collected, and from these the attempt is made to present a picture of humanity's development. Although materials, external facts, were of enormous importance for Herman Grimm, they were nonetheless not at all the main thing. He often entertained the thought: Could it not be that for some epoch or other precisely the most significant documents, the decisive ones, have disappeared without a trace — lost, so that one actually passes by the truth most of all in focussing too conscientiously and exactly on the documents? Hence, he was convinced that, in abiding most faithfully by external documents, one is least of all capable of providing a true picture of human development. Only a falsified picture could arise in keeping strictly to external documents alone.

However, something else has arisen in the cultural life of humanity. What took place outwardly, what happened has, thanks to leading individualities, undergone a spiritual rebirth. This is evidenced by personalities who have transformed it artistically, who have utilized it for cultural purposes. Thus, in looking back for instance to the time of ancient Greece, Herman Grimm said to himself: Some documents exist concerning this Greek age, but these are insufficient to enable one to understand the Greek world. Yet what the Greeks experienced has found its rebirth in the works of Greek art, has been re-enlivened by significant Greek personalities. Immersing oneself in them, letting the Greek spirit affect one, a truer picture of the Greek world is attained than in merely assembling external facts. In this way, the facts themselves disappeared, so to say, for Herman Grimm. One is inclined to say, they melted away from his world-picture. What remained in his world-picture was a continuous stream of what he called the creations of "folk-phantasy."

In contemplating *Julius Caesar*, for example, he not only took account of the historical documents, he considered what *Shakespeare* had made of Caesar as of equal significance, comparable to what is contained in the existing documents. Through characteristic human beings he looked back at the age in question. For Herman Grimm, the course of humanity's development became something always handed on from one personality to another, seeing it as a spiritual process encompassed by what he termed creative phantasy. Proceeding from this point of view, he sought to gain a picture of the creative folk-phantasy at work in western culture — a sense of the actual course of events in the development of humanity, so as to be able to say: The epochs of western culture follow one upon the other, supersede each other — from the earliest epochs up to the present, i.e., from the oldest times to which he wished to return, up to his own period, the age of Goethe. They therefore represent an ongoing stream, the influence of folk phantasy within western cultures.

Starting out from this urge, he turned his attention early on to that grandiose phenomenon of western cultural life, Homer's "Iliad." This occupied him for a period of time during the 1890s, leading to his truly exemplary book, *Homer*. One gladly takes up this volume again and again in wanting, from a modern viewpoint, to immerse oneself in the beginnings of the Greek world. Adopting his general standpoint, it shows us Herman' Grimm from another side. His gaze is directed to the world of the gods as depicted in Homer's

"Iliad" — to the battling Greek and Trojan heroes, and the question arises for him: How do matters actually stand with regard to this interplay of the world of the gods with the normal human world of warring Greek and Trojan heroes? This becomes a question for him. It is indeed striking, what a tremendous difference there is in the Homeric portrayal, between the humans walking around and the nature of those beings described as immortal gods. And Herman Grimm attempts to present the gods in Homer's sense as portraying, so to say, an "older" class of beings wandering on the earth. Even if Herman Grimm, in his more realistic way, sees these beings as "human beings," he does look back into a culture that in Homer's time had long lost its significance, a culture that had been superseded by another, to which the Greek and Trojan heroes belong. Thus, Herman Grimm has an older and a younger class of humanity play into one another in Homer's "Iliad;" and what has remained over of real effects of a class of beings that had lived previously, enters for Herman Grimm (in Homer's sense) into what takes place between Greece and Troy.

Herman Grimm saw the further progress of humanity in this way — as a continual supplanting of older cultural cycles by newer ones and an interplay of older cycles with newer ones. Each new cultural cycle has its task, that of introducing something new into the general development of humanity. The old remains extant for a while and still interacts with the new.

It can be said that what Herman Grimm investigated, to the extent possible in the last third of the nineteenth century, has now to be set forth once more from the point of view of spiritual science. He did not look further back than the Greek age. For this reason, he was unable to arrive at what recent spiritual research describes in looking to the lofty, purely spiritual beings of primeval antiquity, exalted above the human being. He did, however, frequently touch upon results of recent spiritual research — as nearly as anyone can without conducting such research themselves.

In going back to earlier stages in the development of humanity, we attempt, in spiritual research, to show that we do not arrive at the animal species in the sense of the Darwinian theory that is interpreted materialistically nowadays. Rather, we attempt to show that we come to purely spiritual ancestors of the human being. Prior to the cycle of humanity in which human souls live in physical bodies, there is another cycle of humanity in which human beings did not yet incorporate themselves in physical bodies. Herman Grimm leaves the question undecided, so to say, as to what was actually involved with the "gods," before human beings stepped onto the earth. However, he does recognize the ordered sequence of such cycles of humanity. And this results in an important point of contact with what spiritual science presents. That he takes account of such regular periodic stages taking place brings him especially close to us.

He attempts to extend his spiritual observations over three millennia. The first millennium for him is the Greek millennium. With Herman Grimm, one is inclined to say, there is something like an undertone in his manner of characterizing the Greeks, as though he were to say: In looking to the Greeks, they do not appear constituted like human beings of today, particularly in the oldest periods. Even someone like *Alcibiades* [ca. 450-404 B.C.] appears to us like a kind of fairy-tale prince, it is as though one beheld what is superhuman. Still, out of this Greek world that, as already mentioned, Herman Grimm presents as being altogether unlike the later human world, there towers all that arose in the subsequent Greek world and in what follows, becoming the most important constituent of our cultural life. And finally, at the end of the first thousand years contemplated by Herman Grimm, the most significant impulse in humanity's development stands before his soul: the Christ impulse.

Herman Grimm is sparing in what he has to say about the figure of Christ, just as he is restrained in various other matters. But the occasional observations he makes show that he would as little go along with those who would "dissolve" Christ, as it were, to the point of a mere thought impulse, as he would go along with those who want to see Christ Jesus only in human terms. He emphasizes that two kinds of impulses actually proceed from the figure of Christ — one of colossal strength, that continues to work on throughout the further development of humanity — and the other impulse which consists in immense gentleness. Herman Grimm sees the entire second millennium of western cultural development taking shape in such a way that the Greek world is as though absorbed by the Christ impulse and the resulting mixture of Christianity and Greekness is incorporated into the Roman world, overcoming it. Out of this something quite unique arises. That is his second millennium, the first Christian millennium. The Roman element is not the main thing for him, but rather the Christian impulses. Everything of a political or external nature disappears for Herman Grimm in this millennium. He looks everywhere at how the manifold Christ impulse makes itself felt. His conception of Christ is neither narrow nor small, but broad. When a book on the life of Jesus, *La Vie de Jésus* [1863], by Ernest Renan was published, Herman Grimm referred to it in the periodical he edited at the time, "Künstler und Kunstwerke" [Artists and Works of Art]; he attempted to show how pictorial representations of the Christ figure had undergone changes over the centuries both in the visual arts and in literature. He sought to demonstrate how the Christ impulse undergoes changes. He pointed out that people had always conceived of the Christ impulse according to their own outlook. In Ernest Renan he saw an instance of someone in the nineteenth century who conceived of Christ once again in a narrow sense only.

In Herman Grimm's view, Christianity needed about a thousand years to send its impulses into the rivulets and streams of western spiritual life. Then came the third millennium, the second Christian one, in which we still find ourselves today. It is the millennium at the dawn of which spirits such as *Dante* and *Giotto* arose, as also artists like *Michelangelo, Leonardo da Vinci, Raphael* and so on, followed by the works of *Shakespeare* and *Goethe*. These cycles in the development of humanity, an ongoing stream, he spoke of as an expression of the being of creative phantasy. Again and again Herman Grimm sought to present in lectures given to his students, this rhythmically subdivided, ongoing stream of humanity's development. Herman Grimm aimed to show how single creations had their place within the unbroken flow.

Thus, for him, Michelangelo, along with Raphael, Savonarola, Shakespeare and others, such as Goethe, were in a manner of speaking the spiritual constituents that become explicable on seeing them against the background of the ongoing stream of creative phantasy.

For Herman Grimm this was especially apparent at the source, in the ninth or the tenth century before our era, with Homer. Thus, Herman Grimm addresses himself in an immediate way to the human soul, in drawing our attention to a specific work of art — be it Raphael's “'Marriage of Mary and Joseph,” a painting of the Madonna, or one of the creations of Leonardo da Vinci, or later, of Goethe. He grants us the feeling of standing as though directly within the unique qualities of the particular work. In considering with him the arrangement of colours, the figures and their gestures, while standing inwardly before the work of art, there emerges for us something like a tableau of the entire progress of humanity — now called forth by a single entity in that onward-flowing, all-encompassing stream of creative phantasy — over three millennia.

Thus, with Herman Grimm, one is first conducted into the intimate aspects of the work of art in question and is then led up to the summit from which the total stream can be surveyed. However, that is not something he considered in a theoretical manner. It seemed entirely natural for Herman Grimm to look at the totality of the onward flowing spiritual stream of humanity's development in this way. As he explained it to me at a midday meal, as mentioned, with his whole soul he actually lived, as a matter of course, within this spiritual stream, and he could not look at a single phenomenon in any other way than as though it were excerpted from this mighty stream of humanity's development.

The whole of western cultural development, seen as folk phantasy, stood before his soul, though not as a general abstract idea, but filled with real content. He saw himself as inwardly connected with this luminous content extending over millennia, such that everything he wrote appears to one as individual segments of an enormous work. Even in only reading a book review by Herman Grimm, one has the impression as though it were cut out from a colossal work setting forth the whole development of humanity. One feels oneself positively placed before such a colossal work, having opened it, and as though one were reading a few pages in it. It is the same with an article or an essay by Herman Grimm. And one comprehends how Herman Grimm could say of himself, in the evening of his life, in writing the preface to his collection of *Fragments*, that the idea had floated before him of a portrayal of the ongoing stream of folk phantasy, and that therein the whole of western culture had appeared to him. A particular subject he had pursued appeared as if it had been taken out of a finished work. However, he placed no more value on what had been printed than on what he had only written down, and on what he had written down, no more value than on what lived in his thoughts.

In referring to this, I should like to add a further

impression, without putting it into an abstract formula — having been fond of Herman Grimm, remaining so, and in valuing his work and the kind of person he was: Herman Grimm was never able to reach the point of actually carrying out what stood before his mind's eye as something so beautiful, so colossal, so magnificent that even his works on Homer, on Raphael, on Michelangelo, on Goethe, appear to us as fragments of this comprehensive, unwritten work. We read the lines of the introduction to the *Fragments* mentioned above with a certain feeling of wistfulness. He states there that, though it would most likely not come about, it would perhaps be feasible to rework into a book what he had to say to his students year after year — and newly revised every year — concerning the progression of European cultural life in the last form these lectures took. One reads these lines today the more wistfully, as it did indeed not come to such a rewriting. We had to see Herman Grimm pass away, knowing what lived in his soul, intended for present-day culture — having this sink with him into the grave.

We have characterized the sweeping cultural horizons underlying Herman Grimm's written works. Spiritual science aims to show what can be gained in widening one's spiritual horizons. It can be said that for the purpose of gradually entering into the whole outlook inherent in spiritual research, anyone immersing himself in Herman Grimm's spirit has the finest precepts. Apart from the breadth of his horizons, we see how he approached the phenomena, how his thoughts and feelings led him to everything he wrote in his comprehensive works on Homer, Raphael, Michelangelo and Goethe. And, bearing in mind what is set forth in his other writings, one sees that Herman Grimm distinguishes himself in significant ways from other spirits, in possessing attributes belonging to the kind of soul-deepening we have spoken of in describing the path the soul has to take in order to enter the spiritual worlds.

We have stressed that for the spiritual path, the intensity of soul-forces has to become greater. Deeper soul-forces are to be called forth that otherwise slumber. Inner strength, inner courage and boldness are required to a greater extent than in ordinary life; concepts are to be grasped more sharply. The soul needs to identify itself more fully with its own being, with the forces of thinking, feeling and willing. Initial signs of this are evident everywhere with Herman Grimm, by which he was, for example, in a position to describe works of art in such an intimate and personal way, as in the case of Raphael and Michelangelo. This is a precursor, however, to further illuminating the spiritual world. The basis of Herman Grimm's historical research does not lie in what is nowadays called "objectivity," but in his allying himself with the cultural phenomena he portrays, as accords with the spiritual world. In this way, wholly forgetting itself and yet in a rare sense conscious of itself, the soul immerses itself in the corresponding cultural manifestation.

This becomes particularly evident when he directs his attention to a single cultural phenomenon such as Raphael, elevating this to the overall stream of human spiritual life. His impressions then become bold, powerful ideas — and what others do not venture to say with the same shade of feeling, or with the same subtlety of ideas, Herman Grimm does venture, becoming in this way a representative of the spirit. And he then stands before us with such boldness that we are sometimes reminded of the Gospel writers. It is just that they wrote more in keeping with mysticism, while Herman Grimm wrote in the sense of a modern spiritual discourse. Just as the Gospels reach upward to attain the horizon of mankind as a whole, so Herman Grimm reaches upward with his Raphael book to the horizon of mankind as a whole.

It is miraculous when, in his audacious way — seemingly tearing his soul out of himself and striding as though alongside Raphael — as in an overall stream of evolution — he erupts in words that can truly tell us more than any mere presentation of world history: "Raphael is a citizen of world-history. He is like one of the four rivers that according to the belief of the ancient world flowed out of Paradise."

In letting such a sentence duly affect one, Herman Grimm's perception of Raphael takes on an altogether different character, compared to what other authors have to say. Hence, for Herman Grimm, the various personalities of history merge into the overall stream of spiritual life. It could also be said, he brings the highest spiritual spheres down to the personal element. And in speaking the following heartfelt words, Herman Grimm further expresses his relation to leading cultural figures:

"If, by some miracle, Michelangelo were called from the dead, to live among us again, and if I were to meet him, I would humbly stand aside to let him pass; if Raphael came by, I would follow him, to see whether or not I might have the opportunity of hearing a few words from his lips. With Leonardo and Michelangelo one can confine oneself to reporting what they once were in their day; with Raphael one has to start from what he is for us today. Concerning the two others, a slight veil has passed over them, but not over Raphael. He belongs among those whose growth is as yet far from being at an end. We may imagine that Raphael will present ever new riddles to future generations of humanity." [*Fragments*, Vol. II, p.170]

This counts as a characteristic mood, rather than as something objective in the sense of what is normally demanded nowadays. But it does describe matters in such a way that we feel ourselves transposed, in an immediate way to what had lived in Herman Grimm's soul in writing such sentences. It becomes understandable that such a spirit had to struggle in coming to terms with such a world-historical figure as Raphael. Oddly, as he himself relates, it was quite different for him, in describing the life of Michelangelo. The portrayal of the life of Michelangelo by Herman Grimm is a marvellous document, though in some respects perhaps, it counts today as having been surpassed. Seen against the background of the life of that time, the figure of Michelangelo stands out significantly from other figures — as also from the unique description of the city of Florence. Herman Grimm places a tableau before us in contrasting two spiritual entities, Athens and Florence. With that, the weaving together of three millennia as characterized by Herman Grimm, appears as a mighty background upon which Dante and Giotto appear, along with other painters of that time — followed by figures such as Savonarola, and finally Michelangelo himself.

It becomes evident that Herman Grimm responded differently to Raphael and his surroundings than to Goethe, while presenting everything with no less familiarity. In the case of Herman Grimm's Goethe portrayal, we sense everywhere that he had grown up as a spiritual descendant of Goethe. With his Michelangelo portrayal, we feel how he enters into everything personally, wandering the streets, visiting every palace in Florence. Besides personally acquainting himself with other matters, he succeeds in standing as it were before Michelangelo, and in depicting his actual manner of working. All this is as though cast from the same mould.

This differs from what he presents concerning Raphael. There we sense a wrestling with the material, with the spiritual image of Raphael. It is as though Herman Grimm were never able to achieve satisfaction. He describes having taken up the material again and again, while nothing appeared adequate to him of what he had already published. That was true even of his last works — of what he finally attempted as a portrayal of Raphael's personality. This remained a fragment, appearing in the collection of essays entitled *Raphael as a World Power*, from which the sentences derive that were just read out.

Why did Herman Grimm struggle with the material, precisely in the case of Raphael? It is because he could only present something to his own satisfaction in uniting himself completely with the material. In Raphael, however, he saw a spirit characterized in the words quoted: "Raphael is a citizen of world-history. He is like one of the four rivers that, according to the belief of the ancient world, flowed out of Paradise." And thus, with every statement applied to him, Raphael grew to giant size. Herman Grimm could never be satisfied, since he could not capture this "world-power" in a book. If the comprehensive breadth and grace of his spirit is evident in the portrayals of Homer, Michelangelo and Goethe, with his Raphael discourse we see the profound uprightness, the profound honesty of Herman Grimm's personality.

Whoever takes up his book on Homer will possibly find it not scholarly enough. But Herman Grimm states on the very first page, that this book is not meant to be a contribution to Homer research. As already set forth here, Herman Grimm could conduct himself in this and similar matters much like a spiritual "lord." Thus, it appears quite natural that, in collecting his ideas on Goethe for publication, he boldly started out from the view that every other book he had come across concerning Goethe fell short. What seems like brazenness to some, can be taken for granted in the context of his literary and artistic abilities.

That is how he relates to everything in cultural life. Hence for those who adhere to the standpoint of erudite scholars, Herman Grimm's Homer book may seem intolerable. All the many questions that have been raised concerning Homer — whether or not he actually lived, whether the "Iliad" was put together from so and so many details, and so forth — all that did not concern him. He took it as it was. In this way, however, it became clear to him how wonderfully it is composed, how what comes later always refers to what preceded it. Everything that shows this inherent composition appears to us as inwardly coherent. But apart from that, what appears most salutary for a spiritual researcher is his immersion in the soul-life of the Homeric heroes. Everywhere, we see Herman Grimm's soul-imbued style extend to the soul-life of Homer's heroes. Everywhere we see the Achilles-soul comprehended, the Agamemnon-soul, the Odysseus-soul, and so on. As a description of souls, this book is overpowering in its effect, in spite of the familiarity of the stylistic presentation! We are led not only to the heights of historical contemplation, but also deep into the souls of the single Homeric figures. Some scholars will inevitably say, Herman Grimm has taken the "Iliad" at face value, with disregard for the whole of Homer research and all preliminary study, accepting it verse for verse! Indeed, he does so — quite "amateurishly" — and the dry conclusion could then be: There someone has written a book without any preliminary study.

Did Herman Grimm in fact write this book without any preliminary study? Anyone concerning himself with the works of Herman Grimm will find the preliminary studies, only they look different from the preliminary studies of the usual experts. The preliminary studies of Herman Grimm lay in soul studies, in immersing himself in the secrets of the human soul. And one can convince oneself that no one could have shed such light on the Homeric heroes. without those preliminary studies. Herman Grimm looks for what held sway in Homer's phantasy. But what he says reveals him to be the finest knower of human souls. We may expect remarkable things of him in considering the way he viewed Homer's heroes — from Achilles to Agamemnon to Odysseus. How did he find the words to write, in his Homer book and other works, what can seem to the researcher so uncommonly spiritual? He was able to do so on account of quite definite preliminary studies. And these are to be found among the works of Herman Grimm's first period.

Above all, we have the wonderful collection of novellas [1862] that is perhaps less read today than other modern products of its kind. However, these *should* be read by those who take an interest in spiritual things. As a collection of novellas, it is an intensive attempt to get to know human souls, to fathom human secrets and the soul's activity beyond the physical plane. The first of these novellas, "The Singer," belongs to Herman Grimm's earliest phase as an author. In this work it is shown how a man acquires a deep, passionate yearning for a woman of a broad spiritual nature. However, these two personalities are never able to come together. The woman sends this ardent man away from her social circle, while everything lives on in the man's soul in the way of impulses that drew him to her. On the other hand, what proceeds from his soul saps at his bodily strength. Set forth as corresponds to spiritual research, we see him gradually destabilized in his soul. He is taken in by a friend to live on his estate, becoming, however, entangled again in the woman's "net." The friend recognizes that it is high time to fetch this person his friend adheres to so completely. She does come — but too late. Whereas she is actually in front of the house, the individual concerned shoots himself.

And now comes something, taken up unreservedly in spiritual research, which Herman Grimm so often touches upon in artistic expression, but allows to devolve into indefiniteness. Briefly and succinctly he describes how, in the singer's imagination the deceased lives on. The scene is unforgettable in which, feeling her entire guilt in the death of this man, she sees him approaching from the realm of the dead, night after night. This now fills the content of her soul. It is not described as being a mere figment of her imagination, but in the sense of someone who knows there are secrets that reach beyond the grave. It is a wonderful description, that tells how the friend plants himself in front of the woman when she says the deceased comes to her — continuing right up to her final letter to the friend, in which she expresses that she herself now feels close to death. For her, the deceased, to whom she was so closely bound, had drawn her towards him from the realm of the dead. Probably no modern author has found the right tone, in touching on the spiritual world with such sincerity.

In spiritual research we present how, in going through the portal of death, what otherwise always remains united with the human being — also in sleep — the so-called etheric body, raises itself along with the higher soul-members, out of the physical body, passing over into the spiritual world. In the field of spiritual research, we draw a picture of how the corpse remains behind and how the human being with his ether body loosens himself, step by step, one member after the other, from the physical body. The etheric body is then for a time the enclosure for the higher soul-members of the human being. That is an idea with which those who approach closer to spiritual research can become more and more conversant. In what follows we shall be able to consider in what an admirable way the artistic soul of Herman Grimm touches upon these facts of the spiritual world. This will lead us again to the question as to why, for deeper reasons, Herman Grimm did not develop his cultural discourse into a comprehensive work.

Apart from his novella, Herman Grimm wrote a

further work, a novel, *Unüberwindliche Mächte* [1867], [Insurmountable Powers], in which, as with his work in general, his refined style leads us to a contemplation of the world and of life. Particularly remarkable is what might be called the clash of two cultures in miniature. The one world adheres to title, status and rank. Deriving from an old lineage, an impoverished count lives in the afterglow of his hierarchical status. Wonderfully contrasted in this novel is the way in which the world of old prejudices and rankings encounters the New World. The quite different views and notions of America play into this. The individual identifying himself with hierarchical prejudices, whom Herman Grimm calls *Arthur*, encounters Americans. He meets *Emmy*, the daughter of Mrs. Forster, who has grown up with American values. We see this count passionately enraptured by Emmy.

It would be impossible even to outline the rich content of this novel adequately. We encounter the whole contrast of Europe and America. In addition, there is the contrast of the old Prussian milieu and the newly constituted Prussian milieu arising as the outcome of wars. It is a tremendous cultural "painting" in which the characters are featured, and from which they emerge. Only this much can be indicated: that, as a result of the confluence of these streams, Arthur, the count, dies a tragic death right before he was to marry

Emmy. A deluded relative considers himself the rightful heir to the count's lineage, seeing the count as a bastard. Stung with envy and jealousy, he opposes the count, and on the eve of his marriage, the count is shot down by this individual.

Someone wanting to contemplate this novel merely rationalistically might consider it as concerned with the unbridgeable prejudice of social standing. However, the expression "insurmountable powers" can perhaps hardly seem more justified than when Herman Grimm, unintentionally indicates the idea of karma, the idea of the causal connection of destinies in human life — as though knotted together one after another. We see him depict forces at work in destiny that can only come into play in working over from earlier embodiments — from previous earth-lives. He does not describe this in speaking theoretically of "forces" or of "karma," but in simply letting the facts speak for themselves, giving expression to these powers that then appear in a manner corresponding to the ideas of spiritual research. We see a karmic destiny unfold; we see insurmountable karmic powers come to expression. And we see something further:

Emmy remains behind. The final glance that fell into Arthur's eyes as he lay there, his heart shot through, was when she bent over him and their eyes met in a certain expression. An utterance of Herman Grimm remains unforgettable, in saying, the spirit gave way at the moment his eyes assumed the peculiarity of appearing as no more than physical instruments. But now we encounter once more Herman Grimm's penetration of worlds that lie beyond death — what one would like to call his chaste penetration of worlds out of which souls work on, in remaining real once they have gone through the portal of death.

In a brief concluding chapter, Herman Grimm shows us Emmy gradually becoming infirm. It is entirely characteristic of his close connection to matters of soul and spirit, that he describes Emmy's approaching death. She is brought to Montreux. Montreux and its surroundings are uniquely described. However, Herman Grimm does not describe Emmy's passing like authors who have no relation to spiritual matters, but rather as someone taking account of how the secrets of death, of the realm beyond, speak to the soul. I would render something incomplete if I did not add in conclusion Herman Grimm's own words on the death of Emmy:

"This was Emmy's dream.

Between midnight and morning, she believed she woke up.

Her initial glance at the window, through which a pale light streamed in, was free and clear and she knew where she was. She also heard her mother, who slept next to her, breathing. However, a moment later, with a sense of pressure she had never felt before, overwhelming anxiety overcame her. It was no longer the thoughts that had tormented her during the last few days, but as though a giant hand were holding all the world's mountains over her by a thin thread, and that at any moment the fingers holding them could loosen, and the whole mass would fall down on her, to remain lying on her eternally. Her eyes wandered hither and thither looking for a glimmer of light, but there was none; the light of the window extinguished, her mother's breathing no longer audible and stifling loneliness all around, as though she would never come alive again. She wanted to call out, but could not; she wanted to touch herself, but not a limb obeyed her. All was completely silent, completely dark; no thoughts could be grasped in this frightful, monotonous anxiety. Even memory was taken from her — and then, at last a thought returned: Arthur!

And wondrously now, it was as if this one thought had transformed itself into a point of light that became visible to the eyes. And to the extent the thought grew to become boundless longing, this light grew, spreading out, and suddenly, as though it sprang apart and unfolded itself, it took on form — *Arthur stood before her!* She saw him, she recog-

> nized him at last. It was surely he himself. He smiled and was close beside her. She did not see whether he was naked, nor whether he was clothed: but it was him, she knew him too well; it was he himself, no mere phantom that had taken on his form."

Thus, Herman Grimm has the one who has long since gone through the portal of death approach her, now a seeress; at the moment of her death she approaches the deceased, addressing his soul: "She did not see whether he was naked, nor whether he was clothed: but it was him, she knew him too well; it was he himself, no mere phantom that had taken on his form."

> "He stretched out his hand to her and said, 'Come!' Never had his voice sounded as sweet and enticing as now. With all the strength she was capable of, she tried to raise her arms towards him, but she was unable to do so. He came still nearer and stretched out his hand closer to her, 'Come!' he said again.
>
> For Emmy it was as though the power with which she attempted to bring at least a word over her lips, would have been capable of moving mountains, but she was not able to say even this one word.
>
> Arthur looked at her, and she at him. With only

the possibility of moving a finger, she would have touched him. And now, most terrible of all: he appeared to shrink back again! 'Come!' he said for the third time. Sensing he had spoken for the last time, that the terrible darkness would break in again upon his heavenly gaze, filled now with a fear that tore at her as frost splits trees, she made a final attempt to raise her arms to him. It was impossible to overcome the weight and the cold that held her captive — but then, as a bud bursts open, from which a blossom grows before our eyes, there grew out of her arms, other shining arms, out of her shoulders, gleaming new shoulders. And lifting these arms toward Arthur's arms, his hands grasping her hands while he floated slowly backwards, drawing her after him, the whole magnificent figure rose with him, out of Emmy's."

The emergence of the etheric body out of the physical body cannot be described more wonderfully, in having been thus approached by a pure artist-soul. That was a spirit, that was a soul that lived in Herman Grimm, of which we may say that it came close to what we seek so eagerly in spiritual research. Herman Grimm provides evidence that, in approaching the twentieth century, the modern human being sought paths to spiritual life.

So we turn gladly to Herman Grimm, wanting only

to continue further on the same path. We see him elevate the creations of Raphael, the creations of Michelangelo, the experiences of Goethe, the Greek-soul of Homer, to the stream that he sees flowing onward as "creative phantasy" through millennia. We then know how close Herman Grimm was, in his entire feeling and perception, to what lives and weaves as the soul-spiritual behind all physical reality. For when Herman Grimm refers to his "creative phantasy" we are not dealing with total abstraction. In so far as it is still perhaps a matter of residual abstraction, to that extent it can seem necessary to break through the thin wall separating Herman Grimm from the living spirit, effective not only as creative phantasy, but living as immediate spiriteffective behind the entire sense world. It could appear a form of unwarranted restraint, to say no more than Herman Grimm in speaking of the continual onward working of the phantasy of humanity. After all, as an artist, he touched so intimately on the soul that lives on, in having gone through the portal of death. Hence, it will not be difficult for us, where Herman Grimm speaks of "creative phantasy," to see the living spirit that, as spiritual researchers, we seek behind the sense world.

Perhaps it will not seem unjustified to assert that, for a spirit that struggled so honestly and uprightly for truth — wanting to approach this creative phantasy ever and again — it was, in the end, too much of an abstraction for him. It urged him to grasp the living spiritual element, and for that reason the great work he intended could not come about — since if it had been written, it would have had to become a work that portrayed the spiritual world not merely as creative phantasy, but as a world of creative beings and individualities.

Spiritual research has not been placed into the modern age arbitrarily. It is demanded by seeking souls of our time — seeking souls to whom, as we have seen, Herman Grimm so clearly and characteristically belongs. In this way we can become aware that with spiritual research we do not stand as alien and isolated in modern cultural life. We have been able to look to Herman Grimm as to a related spirit. Even if he does not share the same view completely, we do nonetheless stand — or can at least stand, immeasurably near to him. It is better to contemplate such a figure as a whole rather than scrutinizing every detail — to look at the harmony of soul with which Herman Grimm can affect us, his mildness and then again keenness and strength of soul, with which he can likewise affect us. We may treat this or that question differently from Herman Grimm, but I know that it is not altogether out of keeping with his style, if I summarize what I actually wanted to say in the following words: One could arrive at the thought — let us call it for that matter a delusory thought, one that could be entertained as a beautiful illusion: If higher spirits, other-worldly spirits wanted to acquaint themselves with what happens on the earth by means of reading, they would want to read such writings as those in which Herman Grimm depicts the earthly destinies of human beings.

This feeling can reverberate as though from almost every line of Herman Grimm's writings, raising one up to a sphere beyond the earth. One then feels so akin to this personality that, in characterizing what has been said today concerning Herman Grimm, a beautiful saying could come to mind that he himself employed with reference to his friend *Treitschke* [Heinrich von Treitschke, German historian, 1834-96] whom he valued so much.

"With what existential joy did this human being stand in life. What courage he showed in battle! What a gift he had for language. How new his latest book! How little could anyone take exception to his 'elbows' in expounding his ideas. They too will join in declaring: 'Yes, he was one of ours!'"

These words are at the same time the last words that Herman Grimm wrote and had printed, as we know from the publisher of his works, *Reinhold Steig*. And I should like also, in conclusion, to summarize this evening's considerations with the words: With what existential joy did Herman Grimm stand in life; how mild he was and yet how individual! How little can even they distance themselves from him, if they but understand themselves aright, who differ from him in some way. And, whatever their field of investigation, how closely allied to him must they feel who seek paths to the spirit! What kinship to him must they sense when his amiable figure stands before them — prompting them to break out in the words: *Yes, he was one of ours!*

Translated by Peter Stebbing,
Easter, 2019

Selected Works of Herman Grimm in English

- *Life of Michael Angelo* by Herman Friedrich Grimm. Translated by Fanny Elizabeth Bunnet. Little, Brown, & Co., Boston.
- *The Life and Times of Goethe* by Herman Friedrich Grimm. Little, Brown, & Co., Boston.
- *Correspondence between Ralph Waldo Emerson and Herman Grimm* by Ralph Waldo Emerson. Port Washington, Kennikat Press [1971].
- Herman Grimm, *The Life of Raphael*, translated by Sarah Holland Adams, De Wolfe, Fiske & Co., Boston.

Available in German:

- *Novellen*. Berlin 1856 (Nachdruck Verlag Zbinden 1966).
- *Homers Ilias*. 2 Bde. Hertz, Berlin 1890/95.
- *Goethe. Vorlesungen* gehalten an der Kgl. Universität zu Berlin. 2 Bände. Cotta, Stuttgart 1923.

About the translator

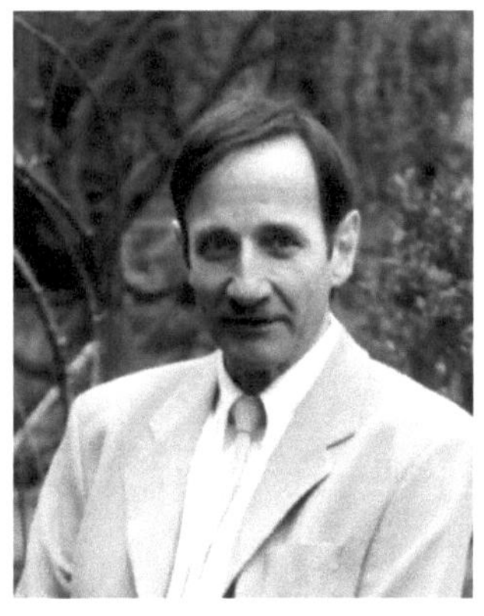

Born in Copenhagen, Denmark in 1941, Peter Stebbing attended Waldorf Schools in England. Having studied at art schools in Brighton and London, he emigrated to the United States in 1966, continuing his studies at Cornell University and earning the M.F.A. degree in painting in 1968.

While teaching design and colour courses over a period of six years in the City University of New York, he began a practical exploration of the scientific colour phenomena set forth by Goethe in his colour theory. This led eventually to a turning point – to the crucial question of finding a corresponding approach to colour in painting.

The new and wholly different training in colour experience begun in 1976 with the painter Gerard Wagner on the basis of Rudolf Steiner's motif sketches, resolved fundamental artistic questions with a coherent and systematic approach. Fully in accord with Goethe's discoveries and method, this approach may be termed "Goetheanistic."

Peter Stebbing subsequently established a painting school at the Threefold Educational Foundation in Spring Valley, N.Y., teaching there from 1983 until 1990. Since 1992 he has been director of the Arteum Painting School (http://www.arteum-malschule.de/) in Dornach, Switzerland. He is also the translator and editor of various anthroposophical art publications.

Other books translated and edited by Peter Stebbing

- Margarita Woloschin, *The Green Snake. An Autobiography.* Floris Books, 2010. 431 pages paperback.
- Elisabeth Wagner-Koch and Gerard Wagner, *The Individuality of Colour. Contributions to a Methodical Schooling in Colour Experience.* 2nd edition. 128 pages. Hardcover. Rudolf Steiner Press, 2009.
- *The Goetheanum Cupola Motifs of Rudolf Steiner. Paintings by Gerard Wagner.* 236 pages. Hardcover. SteinerBooks, 2011.
- *Conversations about Painting with Rudolf Steiner. Recollections of Five Pioneers of the New Art Impulse.* 195 pages, 77 illustrations, hardcover. SteinerBooks, 2008.
- *Three Grimms' Fairy Tales. Paintings by Gerard Wagner.* 70 pages with 31 colour plates, hardcover. SteinerBooks, 2012.
- Rudolf Steiner, *The World of Fairy Tales*. 23 black-and-white shaded drawings by Gerard Wagner. 124 pages, paperback. SteinerBooks 2013.
- *The Art of Colour and the Human Form: Seven Motif Sketches of Rudolf Steiner: Studies by Gerard Wagner*. 218 pages, hardcover. Verlag des Ita Wegman Instituts, 2017. Also available from SteinerBooks, Great Barrington, USA.

On-Line Activities

- On-line *Search* of Bn/GA# 62 texts
- On-line *Compare* of Bn/GA# 62 texts
- Rudolf Steiner Archive & e.Lib: Bn/GA# 62 Overview page
- Wikipedia: the Herman Grimm

www.ingramcontent.com/pod-product-compliance
Lightning Source LLC
LaVergne TN
LVHW052259100826
845147LV00001B/95

* 9 7 8 1 9 4 8 3 0 2 1 5 9 *